The Hidden Secrets of Money

by

Nathan Sloan

Table of Contents

- Introduction

- Secret #1

- Secret #2

- Secret #3

- Secret #4

- Secret #5

- Secret #6

- The 3 Biggest Problems People Have

- The Greatest ROI Activity You Can Do

- The 4 Types of Business

Introduction

I am very excited to be sharing with you principles that have literally not just changed my life, but have been responsible for making millions of pounds for companies that I have worked for.

What I will be revealing in the following pages, is a combination of over one hundred books, courses and seminars that I have paid thousands of pounds to attend and hundreds of hours to learn.

You have in your hands right now, the finished result. This book is the culmination of all the most valuable tips and secrets all laid out ready for you to discover and capitalise on.

I have been very fortunate to have had 1-1 business coaching from some of the world's most successful business owners, combine this with the recent rise of the Internet, it is now easier than ever before to build multiple income streams.

You will notice that this book is quite short, and I have done so for a specific reason.

I did not want to create hundreds of pages of fluff that you get in many other books.

I have been ruthless with the content, deleting large chunks from the original version, and I have only kept in the "essential information" that has been designed to move you from where you are right now, to where you want to be.

Welcome to "The Hidden Secrets of Money". You are about to learn what 95% of people will never know about money.

If you ever wondered why 95% of the world's money is owned by only 5% of the people, then you are going to find this a very valuable read.

You will also learn why most people are struggling financially, living pay check to pay check and unable to ever stop working and even more importantly... what you can do about it.

In the pages below, you will discover why it is very difficult to create "true wealth" and financial independence when you are an "employee" and how you can begin playing the same game as the rich.

You will be learning:

- Why the rich get richer and poor get poorer
- The 3 kinds of income
- How to escape the 9-5 rat race
- How to legally pay less in tax
- What <u>you</u> can do about it

I very excited to share with you what has had such a big impact on my own life. Once I learned these secrets of money, I left a 10 year career and I now make more money than I ever have previously. It's going to be an exciting ride.

I am very happy to now pass these financial secrets on to you so that can then teach your children and closest near ones and dear ones in the hope of a brighter financial future for all.

Sit back, relax and I am sure you will enjoy The Hidden Secrets of Money.

Warm regards,

Secret #1
Money is an effect

The biggest mistake most people make is thinking that they can go out and 'make more money'. They then wonder why they do not have money in their lives.

Money is a result.

What do I mean by this? Let me say it another way. Money is not a cause it is an effect.

It is the by-product of something else.

It can take a few times hearing this for it to make complete sense.

Lets look at it from a different angle. You can't make money the same way that you can't 'lose weight' or 'build muscle'.

If your goal is to "lose weight" then your focus must be on making changes to your diet.

If you want to "build muscle" then you must focus your time and energy on lifting weights.

If you want to "make more money" then you have to create value for someone.

Creating value for someone is what makes money.

You can't make a fire without first putting on logs. Fire does not come before logs.

So what is "value"?

It is benefitting another human being and improving their life in some way.

The more lives you improve, the money you will make. That is the hidden secret that poor people do not understand.

Why do sports stars make so much more money than teachers? Because sports stars make millions of people lives better by providing them with entertainment. Teachers only affect a room full of people.

Is it fair? No, however that is the way it is. When you have your own planet you can do what you want. However while you are on this one, them are the rules.

Richard Branson helps thousands of people travel around the country and the world in comfort with Virgin Trains and Virgin Atlantic.

Bill Gates put a computer, one of the most valuable items ever created in to more homes than anyone else.

When you bought this book, money exchanged hands and you began learning super valuable lessons on how money is really made. Starting to make sense?

Bottom Line: Focus on creating value for people and benefiting people in some way. If done correctly, money will follow as the result.

Secret #2
The 3 Kinds of Income

Did you know that there are actually three kinds of income? 95% of people only know about the first kind, "Earned income" however, there are two more. The 3 types of income are:

Income 1: Earned Income
"<u>You</u> earn your money"

If you have ever worked in a job then you already know about "Earned income". Very simply, this is the kind of income that when you go to work, you get paid for and when you don't go to work, you don't get paid. <u>You</u> earn your money.

The benefit of this kind of income is that it great in the short term as you get paid instantly right after your first month, loverly.

The downside of this type of income is that it is not so good in the medium and long term. This is because in 5 years time, you are still in the same place, living pay check to pay check, unable to ever stop working.
It is also the type of income that is taxed at the <u>highest</u> tax bracket, normally 30-50%. The more money you make, the more you get taxed. Lets move on.

Income 2: Passive Income
"A <u>system</u> makes you money"

The second kind of income is "Passive income" (also known as Residual Income). This is income created by owning a "System" that makes money.

For example, this could be something as small as owning vending machines, to owning rental properties, all the way up to owning your own big business.

The big difference with this type of income is that you do not <u>physically work</u> for this income. It comes to you "passively" by owning the asset.

The benefit of this kind of income is that it can create true financial independence, as you are not "selling time for money".

If you do sell time for money remember, there are only 24 hours in a day and you have a limit on your income.

The downside with kind of income is that it does take serious time and effort to build up.

Income 3: Portfolio Income
"Your money makes you money"

The third kind of income is "Portfolio Income". This is income you receive by owning assets like stocks, bonds, mutual funds and so on.

This type of investment normally pays a "dividend" or by buying low and selling high it can give you income through "capital gains".

The main difference with this type of income is that it is your money that makes you money.

The benefit of this income stream is that you also don't go to work for this money, the money works for you.

The downside of this type of income is that it takes a higher financial knowledge and experience to get started and it also requires some kind of initial investment.

Secret #3
How People Make Money

In today's society, there are <u>four</u> ways in which people make their money. This is either by being an Employee, Self Employed, Business Owner or Investor.

The richest 5% of people in the world are found on the right hand side of this quadrant as business owners and investors and the other 95% of the population are found on the left hand side of the quadrant, as employees and self employed.

Robert Kiyosaki's Cashflow Quadrant

You will notice that people who make <u>earned income</u> are found the left hand side of the quadrant as employee's and self employed.

People who make <u>passive</u> and <u>portfolio</u> income are found on the right hand side of the quadrant, as business owners and investors.

People on the left hand side of the quadrant also pay the most in taxes, even though they make a lot less money. You will find out why this is a bit later on.

People on the right hand side of the quadrant not only earn a lot more money, they also pay tax in a lower tax bracket. Business owners can buy cars, travel, computers, telephones and many other items and write them all off as a "taxable expenses".
It's a double whammy. Don't worry, I'll show <u>you</u> how to benefit from system also later.

Secret #4
The Secret About Tax

If you have ever had a job then you will know about and have paid <u>tax</u>, however, would you like to learn how to pay a lot <u>less</u> in tax leaving more money in your bank account?

The average person pays 30%-50% in income tax alone. The difference is that business owners can easily pay up to <u>40% less</u> in tax.

So this is what this actually means...

3-4 months of the year is spent <u>just paying taxes</u>.

Or

20% of your working life is spent <u>just paying taxes</u>.

Remember This: Tax is your "single biggest expense". The fastest way to make more money, is to <u>reduce your taxes</u>. Please read that last part again as it is very important.

So, if tax is your biggest expense every month, it would be valuable to know how to reduce it and leave more money in your bank account right?

What Exactly IS Tax?

The tax code is <u>not</u> about paying more taxes. Most people do not realise that 99.9% of the tax code has been written to show you how to <u>reduce</u> your taxes.

Before WWII, it was actually only the rich that were taxed. Governments quickly realised that they could change people's behaviour with tax incentives and it is now used for economic growth.

In order to pay less in tax, we need to know and give the government what they want.

Goal of the government: To grow the economy.

To grow the economy, they need people to <u>create jobs</u> and <u>provide housing</u>.

So what this all means is that the tax code is just an "incentive plan" for entrepreneurs and investors to help grow the economy.

How To Legally Pay Less Tax

The reason that business owners and investors are able to pay less in tax is because they play from a different rule book.

Let me show you how this works.

This is what the tax system looks like for everyday employees. It's called earn, tax, spend.

Earn
Tax
Spend

You earn your monthly pay check each and every month. The government then takes their tax cut <u>before</u> you get to see your money and then you get to spend what it left over.

Following me so far?

Well, the rich play by a different set of rules.

Earn
Spend
Tax

When you own a business, you get to earn your money, then you get to <u>spend</u> that money on many tax deductible items like your rent, car, travel, office equipment, clothes and so on, and <u>then</u> you pay tax on what is left over.

On top of that, you pay a <u>lower</u> tax rate on what is left over at the end! The aim of the game then is to spend your money on items that are tax deductible, leaving less money left over to be taxed on.

This is how the rich get richer and the poor get poorer.

Secret #5
Portfolio Theory

This secret is all about becoming an investor.

Investing is all about risk and return. How much risk are you prepared to take which then determines how much return you will be getting on your money.

Normally the two are correlated.

For example, investing in stocks verses investing in bonds.

Over roughly the past 100 years, they've shown an annual return of about 10 percent per year. By contrast, long-term government bonds have returned between 5 and 6 percent.

However stocks are 3x riskier assets. They crash more often and more severe than bonds.

So what is an investor to do?

This is where MPT (modern portfolio theory) comes in. It's basically diversifying across different assets to help spread the risk.

If one investment goes down another might go up to counter balance and minimise the loss, thats the theory.

It is used by the world top billionaire investors.

Let me show you three example portfolios based on the level of risk you are happy to take.

High Risk: High Return

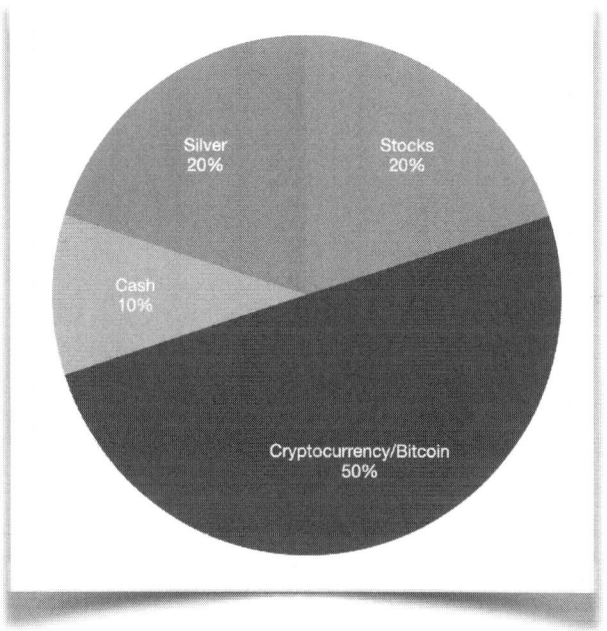

As you can see 50% of your money will be in Bitcoin or some other cryptocurrency. These are extremely volatile however, you get the opportunity for tremendous gains.

The rest of your money is split between stocks and silver which are also riskier than other assets you can own. With only 10% of your money in cash.

Medium Risk: Medium Return

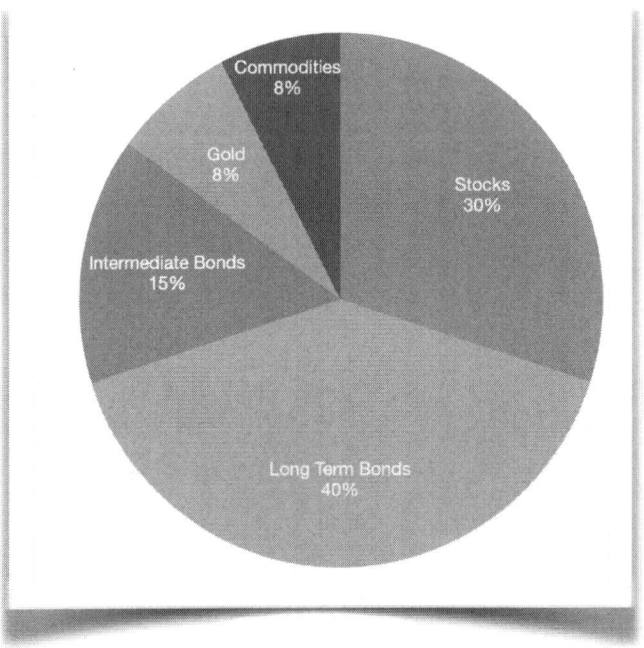

In this scenario you are mostly invested in bonds which are deemed a safe asset class and only 30% in stocks.

You also own some gold and other commodities as a good hedge against market crashes.

Low Risk: Low Return

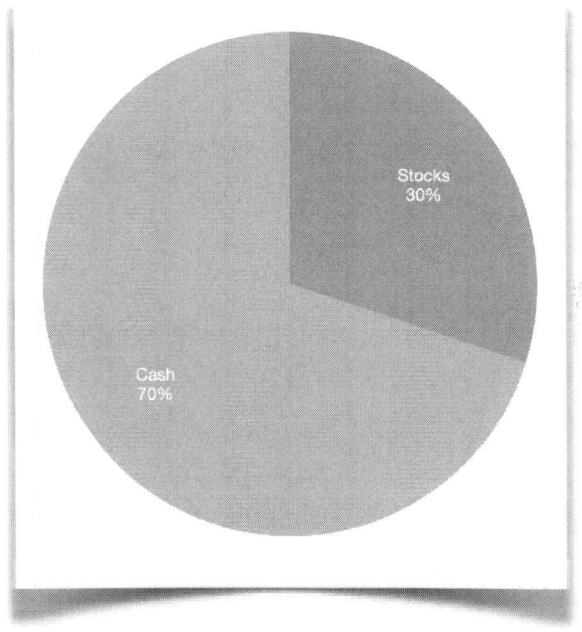

This is how a beginner portfolio might look or for someone who is past 65 years old and doesn't want to take much risk.

Most of your money will be held in cash with only a small amount in the stock market.

So which portfolio is right for you?

It does depend on where you are in life and also how much risk you are prepared to take.

If you are young you could take more risk as even if you lose all your money you have many years to make more.

You may just want to be very conservative and keep most of your money in cash.

Just note that cash is not risk free. Cash loses around 3-5% every year due to inflation so over the long term, it is a bad investment.

This is the reason top investors don't hold a lot of cash. They would rather have their money invested.

Secret #6
How To Escape the 9-5 Rat Race

What exactly is the "Rat Race"?

Basically it is a comparison to the 9-5 job way of life, where you are living pay check to pay check, never able to leave work without everything coming crashing down.

You are spending what you earn each month and have no way of stopping work because your lifestyle is being held up by just <u>one</u> income source, your job.

It is like running on a never-ending hamster wheel which we call the "Rat Race".

If you were to stop working (or get made redundant or injured) then everything would collapse because you only have one income.

What is Financial Freedom?

When you are financially free, you receive your income from a business and/or investments that cover and pay for all your monthly expenses.

Once your income is higher than your expenses then you no longer have to "work" because lifestyle is supported by your "Investments".

How Do I Become Financially Free?

Becoming financially free is the process of converting your "earned income" in to "passive income" in the most efficient way possible.

You would do this by using your excess money from your job each month (your earned income) and start a business on the side.

Once you build a business up to where the income supports you (passive income) you can leave your job and you become financially free.

Earned Income  **Passive Income**

3 Problems Most People Are Not Aware Of

1. Selling Time for Money
The biggest problem most people have is that they do not even realise that they are "selling time for money" which is what is keeping them poor.

The reason for this is simply that this is just something that we all do and have done all our lives. We don't know any different. We follow the crowd. No-one has told us that there is a "better way".

The problem with this is that you can never be financially free selling time for money. There are only 24 hours a day, so you have a limit on your income.

2. Owning Zero Assets
As an employee the harsh reality is that you own and control nothing. It is the owner of the business that owns the asset, the business.

It is the business owner that gets to double their income each year, while you get 2% pay increases.

It is the business owner that makes the passive income and can sell the business at 5x earnings whenever they want.

Even if you work in a business for 40 years of your life... you own <u>nothing</u>.

3. Working in the Rat Race until Age 67
The majority of the population live pay check to pay check not being able to leave work until they are 67 (if they are lucky).

The main reason why people choose this route is because they simply do not know that another option exists.

The good news is that it does not have to be this way. There is another option for you.

So Why Have I Not Been Told This Before?

You may be thinking, why have I not been told this before? It's a very good question. The simple answer is that our economy cannot run without employees.

We need people to be teachers, secretaries, doctors, lawyers, builders, cleaners, waiters and so on. If everyone owned a business and had investments then our way of life wouldn't work and would all collapse.

The important point is that it doesn't have to be <u>you</u>.

What Can I Do About It?

There are basically two main options that you now have.

1. Continue with the 9-5 and retire at 67
2. Learn how to start your own business

Continue with the 9-5 and retire at 67

Your first option is to simply carry on the same route you are now. We would like to point out that there is absolutely nothing wrong with this route. You can live a very good life. We hope you have enjoyed what you have read and learned so far and wish you all the success in the world.

Learn how to start your own business

On the other hand, if you would like to learn how to become the rich that the rules of money have been written for then read on.

The first step is not to feel intimidated or scared about business. Just note that everyone starts from the same place, knowing nothing and having nothing.

All you need at this point is the <u>desire to learn</u>. So why is business the best wealth creating vehicle you will ever have? Let's take a look at the numbers.

The Greatest ROI Activity You Can Do

This is all about the number one place to invest your money to make sure you get the maximum ROI or "return on your investment".

When it comes to investing or wealth creation of any kind, there are many different ways that people can build their wealth. The main avenues are:

- **Business**
- **Stocks**
- **Bonds**
- **Property**
- **Mutual Funds**
- **Commodities**
- **High Interest Saving Accounts**

The reason people invest is simple. To make more money and have their money working for them.

The aim is to get the best ROI (return on investment) that you can right?

What I am about to reveal to you is the number one ROI activity you can do.

In other words, how you can make the maximum amount of money with the minimum amount of time.

Lets look at the investment strategies from above again but this time add in the average return people might get.

Stocks: 10%-20%
Bonds: 1%-10%
Property: 10%-20%
Mutual Funds: 10%
Commodities: 0%-1000%
High Interest Saving Accounts: 0.1%-6%

The average stock trader is classed to be doing very well if they can regularly get a 10% return (ROI).

One of the best investors in the world is Warren Buffet. He is known for being able to consistently get a 20% return from his stock pics.

The majority of people in the world do not invest at all. They will simply keep their money in a high interest savings account like an ISA. This can give you up to a 5% return.

Note: If inflation is over 5% then you are actually losing money and getting poorer, leaving your money in the bank.

This is why pensions are not a great investment at all, however, that is a whole other subject.

So...

Would you like to know what the greatest ROI activity you can do is?

The answer is business, more specifically marketing.

Marketing, when done correctly can give returns in the hundreds of percent consistently on a month to month basis. Nothing else can touch these kinds of returns.

Let me give you a quick and simple example.

Lets say you have 1000 leaflets created about a business event you are holding and it costs you £50 to have them made.

20 people come to the event and 3 people become customers.

Lets say you get a £50 per sale.

This means you make £150. That's a 100% ROI.

Here are the numbers.

Marketing Costs: £50
Sales: £150
Profit: £100
ROI: 100%
Now, this was just a very quick example that was just to make the point. This can be scaled up.

I have worked in businesses where we were spending £4,000 per month on advertising, that was brining in £40,000 worth of sales.

Google spends millions of pounds every month on advertising, but they make hundreds of millions back from it.

The point is this.

Marketing is the greatest ROI activity you can do.

This is the <u>why</u> 93% of millionaires own a business. (you might want to write that statistic down. It's very important to remember).

This is <u>why</u> thousands of people start businesses each year.

So, what does this all mean for you?

The good news is that through business and marketing, you are also going to be able to take your slice of the pie and get your financial goals faster.

So how can you start a business?

I thought you would never ask.

The 4 Types of Business

It's a fact that 93% of millionaires own a business, however, how does someone with no business experience get started?

There are actually <u>four</u> ways in which you can own your own business. Here are the four types of businesses you can start with the pros and cons for each.

1. Create Your Own Brand
"Starting from scratch"

The first kind of business you can start is by "creating your own brand". This is the standard bricks and mortar type business that you normally see on the high street.

Some examples are companies like Virgin, Toyota and Orange.

Here are the pros and cons for this type of business. Starting a business from scratch can cost from £5,000 in to the millions of pounds.

Pros
- High Barrier to Entry
- Can be Very Fast
- Flexibility

Cons
- They Need Investment
- They Are Higher Risk
- 3 Years on average to Profitability

2. The Franchise Business
"The done-for-you business"

The second type of business you can start is the franchise model. Today, you will see many franchises everywhere.

This is because they are a "safer option" compared to starting a business from scratch and they have a higher success rate.
Some of the well known brands are, McDonalds, Starbucks and Specsavers.
They are known as "Turn Key" businesses as someone else has already built the systems and processes for you. 90% has already been done.

You simply pay the start up fee and around 10% of your profit each month to use the brand name.

A franchise can cost anywhere from £100,000 - £5 Million

Pros
- Proven Business Model
- Just Plugin and Go
- Lower Risk

Cons
- You Still Require Start up Investment
- 90% Ownership
- Limited by Location

3. A Network Marketing Business
"The duplication business"

The third kind of business you can start is a network marketing business. This type of business is becoming more and more popular as it can thrive in a bad economy and good economy.

Network marketing is very similar to a franchise where 90% of the business has already been done for you, the only difference is that the products are sold by "word of mouth" and not through a shop.

Network marketing is becoming more popular these days as it is has the lowest start up costs and suits people who have not had any previous business or marketing experience.

The start up costs are normally around £500 - £1500.

Pros
- Lowest Start Up Costs
- Very Low Risk
- No Previous Experience Needed
- 1-12 Months on Average to Profitability

Cons
- Heavy on Friends and Family
- It's a Social Business

4. An Online Business
"a low risk business"

The forth kind of business that you can start is an online business. There are many different types of online business you can start. Here are some of the popular choices.

Affiliate marketing - this is like network marketing where you sell other businesses products for them for a commission.

Sell your own product - if you have your own product or if you have expert knowledge on a particular subject then you can create your own product to sell.

Sell on Amazon/Ebay - many people are choosing to write books (like this one) or buying and selling on Ebay as a business option.

Start a YouTube Channel - Setup a YouTube channel on a topic you know and love and begin making videos. After you get 1000 subscribers you will begin making advertising revenue. From then on you will be making money for every video you create.

Pros
- Lowest Start Up Costs
- Very Low Risk
- No Previous Experience Needed
- 1-12 Months on Average to Profitability

Cons
- Takes More Time
- Can be lonely

The 9-5 Job Is Broken!

One of the biggest problems today is that the 9-5 job is broken. The whole system is set up so that one person wins and everybody else loses.

Here is what I mean.

There is only one person who makes all the money, the business owner. There is only one person who makes passive income, the business owner.

There is only one person who owns the asset at the end of day, the business owner and there is only one person who drives the Porsche, the business owner.

Who gets the opportunity to retire after only 5 years work? Can you guess? That's right, the business owner.

On the flip side...

Who works for Earned income? The employee.

Who pays the most in tax even though they earn less? The employee. Who owns nothing even if they work for the company for 40 years? The employee.

Who doesn't get paid if they take a day off? The employee. Who has to work until they are 67? The employee.

Who is lucky to make 4% more than they did the previous year? That's right...The employee.

However there is an even bigger fundamental point to consider.

Your Boss Is Incentivised To Keep You Poor

Think about this? When you get a pay rise, whose pocket does it directly come out of? Your bosses.

To pay you more money, your boss has to make <u>less</u> money. That is how it works.

Why do you think employers do not like giving pay rises?

Even if they do give you a pay rise, this is why they are normally tiny.

Your boss is "incentivised" to keep you on the lowest money possible as it makes them more money.

Now do you see why the 9-5 job is broken?

The good news

So the big question is...what can I do about it?

Here is the solution.

You can start your own business part time, until you can go full time.

I believe that starting your own business is one of the smartest things you can do with your time and money.

You can do this. With some hard work and perseverance you too can build a business that gives you everything you want out of life.

The good news is that it has never been easier and more accessible to you now that we have the internet.

If you have a computer, you can now access the world.

Good luck.

Printed in Great Britain
by Amazon

85076014R00027